The Art of Ripening Fruits

Joe Harrett

Copyright © 2024 by Joe Harrett.

All rights reserved. No part of this book may be used or reproduced in any form whatsoever without written permission except in the case of brief quotations in critical articles or reviews.

Printed in the United States of America.

For more information, or to book an event, contact :
joe.harrett.publish@gmail.com

Cover design by InkCraft Studio

Contents

1 Introduction 1
    The Importance of Proper Fruit Ripening 1

2 Understanding Ripening: Climacteric vs. Non-Climacteric Fruits 5
    Differences Between Climacteric and Non-Climacteric Fruits 5
    How to Handle These Fruits for Optimal Ripening 7

3 Mastering Ripening Through Strategic Fruit PairingIntroduction 9
    The Best Fruit Combinations for Faster Ripening 9
    Fruit Pairings to Avoid to Prevent Over-Ripening 10
    Balancing Ripening Times Through Fruit Pairing 11

4 Techniques for Perfectly Ripened Fruits: Traditional Methods vs. Modern Tools 13
    The Importance of Proper Fruit Ripening 13
    Modern Tools and Technologies for Fruit Ripening 15

5 Achieving the Perfect Ripeness: Selection, Techniques, and Culinary Uses
.... 19
    How to Select the Right Fruits for Ripening 19
    How to Avoid Over-ripening and Maintain Freshness 23
    Recipes and Uses for Perfectly Ripe Fruits 24

6 Mastering the Storage and Preservation of Ripe Fruits 29
    Best Practices for Storing Ripe Fruits 29
    Techniques to Preserve Freshness 32
    How to Freeze Ripe Fruits for Later Use 35

7 Navigating the World of Ripening: Myths, FAQs, and Common Mistakes
.... 37

Debunking Popular Myths About Ripening 37

Frequently Asked Questions About Fruit Ripening 39

Common Mistakes and How to Avoid Them 40

8. Mastering the Art of Seasonal Fruit Ripening 42

Summer Fruits: How to Combine for Optimal Ripening 42

Autumn Fruits: Tips for Long-Term Freshness 43

Winter Fruits: Ripening Techniques for Cold Weather 44

Spring Fruits: Preparing for Seasonal Bounty 45

9. Celebrating Ripe Fruits: Creative Uses and Delicious Recipes 47

Smoothies and Natural Juices 47

Desserts Featuring Ripe Fruits 48

Tips for Fruit Desserts 50

Preserving Ripe Fruits for Future Use 50

Creative Ideas for Serving and Presentation 51

10 Mastering the Art of Ripening: A Comprehensive Recap and Final Insights 53

Recap of Key Concepts 53

Benefits of Controlled Fruit Ripening 54

Encouragement for Experimentation and Personal Discovery 55

1 Introduction

The Importance of Proper Fruit Ripening

Fruits are among nature's most exquisite gifts, brimming with flavors, nutrients, and vibrant colors that captivate our senses. Yet, anyone who has bitten into a mealy apple or tasted a sour banana can attest that the joy of fruit lies in its ripeness. Proper fruit ripening is not just a matter of preference; it is the critical factor that determines the flavor, texture, and overall enjoyment of fruit. The difference between a perfectly ripe piece of fruit and one that is under- or overripe can be profound, influencing not just taste, but also the fruit's nutritional value and culinary versatility.

For home cooks, gardeners, and food enthusiasts, understanding the nuances of fruit ripening can transform their relationship with food. Imagine serving a dessert where every berry bursts with flavor, or preparing a salad where each slice of mango or avocado is perfectly creamy and sweet. Proper ripening doesn't just happen by chance; it's the result of knowledge, timing, and often, a bit of strategy. This book seeks to demystify the process, offering readers the tools to achieve that perfect moment when fruit is at its peak.

How the Ripening Process Works

To fully appreciate the art of ripening fruits, one must first understand the biological processes that underpin it. Ripening is the stage of fruit development where it transitions from being immature and inedible to mature and palatable. This process involves a complex interplay of chemical and physical changes, including the breakdown of starches into sugars, softening of the fruit's flesh, and the development of characteristic flavors and aromas.

The Transformation

At the core of ripening is the transformation of starches into sugars. In many fruits, like bananas and apples, starches accumulate during the fruit's growth phase. As ripening progresses, these starches are broken down by enzymes into simpler sugars, such as glucose, fructose, and sucrose. This change is why ripe fruits are sweeter and more flavorful than their unripe counterparts.

Simultaneously, the fruit's texture changes. Cell walls, composed of pectin and other polysaccharides, begin to break down under the influence of enzymes like pectinase and cellulase. This breakdown softens the fruit, making it more tender and easier to eat. The firmness of an unripe pear, for example, gives way to a juicy and buttery texture as it ripens.

Color changes also signal ripening. Chlorophyll, the pigment responsible for the green color in many fruits, breaks down as ripening advances, revealing other pigments such as carotenoids and anthocyanins. These pigments contribute to the red, orange, yellow, and purple hues that make ripe fruits visually appealing.

Aromas and Flavors

Aroma compounds, which are essential to the flavor profile of fruits, are another key aspect of ripening. As fruits ripen, volatile compounds responsible for their distinctive aromas are produced in greater quantities. The fragrant smell of a ripe peach or the intoxicating scent of a mango are direct results of these chemical changes.

The development of these flavors and aromas is influenced by the fruit's exposure to environmental factors like temperature and humidity. Therefore, controlling these factors can help in managing the ripening process, ensuring that fruits develop their best possible flavor.

The Role of Ethylene in Fruit Ripening

Central to the ripening process is ethylene, a naturally occurring plant hormone that acts as a signal for the initiation of ripening. Often referred to as the "ripening hormone," ethylene is a gaseous compound that is produced in small amounts by fruits and other parts of plants. Its role in ripening is so pivotal that understanding ethylene's function is key to mastering the art of ripening fruits.

Ethylene's Mechanism of Action

Ethylene is involved in a feedback loop in many fruits. When a fruit begins to ripen, it produces ethylene, which in turn accelerates the ripening process by stimulating the production of more ethylene. This self-propagating cycle is why certain fruits, like apples and bananas, can ripen quickly once they reach a certain stage.

The action of ethylene extends beyond just the fruit that produces it. Ethylene can also influence nearby fruits, causing them to ripen as well. This is why placing a ripe banana in a bag with an unripe avocado can hasten the avocado's ripening. The banana emits ethylene, which permeates the air around the avocado, triggering its ripening process.

Climacteric and Non-Climacteric Fruits

Fruits can be categorized into two broad groups based on their response to ethylene: climacteric and non-climacteric fruits. Climacteric fruits, such as apples, bananas, and tomatoes, show a significant increase in ethylene production as they ripen. This increase is accompanied by a rise in respiration, leading to the rapid development of ripening characteristics.

Non-climacteric fruits, like grapes, citrus fruits, and strawberries, do not exhibit a significant increase in ethylene production or respiration during ripening. These fruits ripen slowly and steadily, often reaching their optimal ripeness while still attached to the plant. For non-climacteric fruits, factors other than ethylene play a more critical role in ripening, making their ripening process more challenging to manage once harvested.

Practical Applications

Understanding the role of ethylene has practical implications for anyone interested in optimizing fruit ripeness. For example, climacteric fruits can be ripened after harvest by exposing them to ethylene. This knowledge is particularly useful for home cooks and gardeners who may want to stagger the ripening of their fruit to avoid waste or ensure that they always have ripe fruit on hand.

On the other hand, knowing that non-climacteric fruits do not respond significantly to ethylene allows for better planning when purchasing or harvesting these fruits. Since these fruits do not ripen much after harvest, it is important to choose fruits that are already at the desired stage of ripeness.

Purpose and Scope of the Book

"The Art of Ripening Fruits" is designed to be a comprehensive guide for anyone interested in mastering the delicate balance of fruit ripening. Whether you are a home cook looking to enhance the flavor of your dishes, a gardener aiming to harvest fruits at their peak, or a food enthusiast eager to deepen your understanding of this fascinating process, this book will provide the insights and tools you need.

Purpose of the Book

The primary purpose of this book is to empower readers with the knowledge and techniques necessary to achieve perfectly ripe fruits consistently. By understanding the science behind ripening, you can take control of the process, ensuring that your fruits are at their most delicious when you eat or serve them.

This book also aims to dispel common myths and misconceptions about fruit ripening. For example, many people believe that all fruits continue to ripen after being picked, or that refrigerating fruits will always prolong their freshness. By providing clear, science-backed information, this book will help you make informed decisions that lead to better results in the kitchen and beyond.

Scope of the Book

The book covers a wide range of topics, from the basic biology of fruit ripening to practical strategies for managing ripeness. The chapters are structured to guide you through the process step by step, starting with foundational concepts and gradually introducing more advanced techniques.

In addition to the scientific principles behind ripening, this book includes practical advice on selecting, storing, and pairing fruits to optimize their ripeness. You will learn how to use ethylene-producing fruits to your advantage, how to store fruits to extend their shelf life, and how to pair fruits with other foods to enhance their flavors.

The scope of this book also extends to the diverse needs of its audience. For home cooks, there are tips on how to time fruit ripeness to coincide with meal preparation. Gardeners will find advice on when to harvest fruits for optimal ripeness and how to manage the ripening of fruits that mature at different times. Food enthusiasts will appreciate the deep dives into the chemistry of ripening and the exploration of how different factors—such as climate, storage conditions, and handling—affect the final outcome.

Ultimately, this book is about celebrating the joy of fruit at its finest. When you understand the art of ripening, you unlock a world of flavors and textures that can elevate your culinary creations and enhance your appreciation for nature's bounty.

2 Understanding Ripening: Climacteric vs. Non-Climacteric Fruits

Ripening is a crucial process that transforms fruits from their initial hard, often bland state into the sweet, aromatic, and flavorful delights we crave. This transformation, while seemingly magical, follows specific scientific principles. To master the art of ripening, it's essential to understand the two primary categories of fruits: climacteric and non-climacteric. This chapter will delve deeply into these categories, exploring their characteristics, providing examples, and offering practical advice on how to handle them for optimal ripening.

Differences Between Climacteric and Non-Climacteric Fruits

Climacteric Fruits: The Star Performers of Ripening

Climacteric fruits are the stars of the ripening process. These fruits continue to ripen after they have been harvested, thanks to their ability to produce and respond to ethylene gas, a plant hormone that accelerates the ripening process. This hormonal action triggers a series of biochemical changes that soften the fruit, enhance its flavor, and develop its aroma.

Key Characteristics:

- **Ethylene Production:** Climacteric fruits produce ethylene, a gas that speeds up their own ripening and can even influence other fruits nearby.

- **Ripening Continuation:** These fruits can ripen even after being picked from the plant, although they will typically reach their peak flavor if left to ripen on the plant.

- **Textural Changes:** The ripening process involves significant changes in texture, from firm to soft, as cell walls break down and pectin dissolves.

Examples of Climacteric Fruits:

- **Apples:** Apples are a classic example of climacteric fruits. They emit ethylene gas, which facilitates their ripening and can influence nearby fruits.

- **Bananas:** Known for their rapid ripening, bananas produce substantial amounts of ethylene, which causes their skin to turn from green to yellow and finally to brown.

- **Avocados:** Avocados will continue to ripen after being picked, making it important to manage their storage carefully to achieve the desired level of softness.

- **Tomatoes:** Though often thought of as a vegetable, tomatoes are technically climacteric fruits. Their ripening is marked by a color change and development of sugars and flavors.

- **Peaches:** Peaches also fall into this category. They soften and become sweeter as they release ethylene and continue to ripen.

Non-Climacteric Fruits: The Independent Ripeness

In contrast to their climacteric counterparts, non-climacteric fruits do not ripen further once harvested. Their ripening process is largely completed while still on the plant, and they do not produce significant amounts of ethylene. For non-climacteric fruits, ripening is closely linked to the time they spend on the plant, and post-harvest ripening is minimal.

Key Characteristics:

- **No Ethylene Production:** These fruits do not produce significant amounts of ethylene and are less responsive to it.

- **Ripening Completion:** Ripening primarily occurs on the plant, so the fruit must be harvested when it has reached its desired level of ripeness.

- **Stable Texture:** Once picked, these fruits generally do not undergo significant changes in texture or flavor.

Examples of Non-Climacteric Fruits:

- **Strawberries:** Strawberries are non-climacteric; they do not continue to ripen after picking. They should be consumed soon after harvest for optimal flavor.

- **Citrus Fruits (e.g., Oranges, Lemons):** Citrus fruits are another example. They reach their peak ripeness on the tree, and their flavor does not improve significantly after harvest.

- **Grapes:** Grapes do not continue to ripen after being picked. They need to be harvested at their peak flavor.

- **Cherries:** Cherries, like grapes, do not ripen further once harvested, so they should be picked at their peak sweetness.

- **Pineapples:** Pineapples also fall into this category. Their sweetness and flavor are fully developed on the plant, and they do not improve much after harvesting.

How to Handle These Fruits for Optimal Ripening

Handling Climacteric Fruits

1. **Monitoring Ethylene Exposure:** Since climacteric fruits produce ethylene, it's crucial to manage their exposure to this gas. For instance, if you want to speed up the ripening of bananas, placing them in a paper bag will concentrate the ethylene and accelerate the process. Conversely, storing them in a cool, well-ventilated area can slow down the ripening if desired.

2. **Temperature Control:** Temperature plays a significant role in the ripening process. Most climacteric fruits ripen best at room temperature. For example, if you have avocados that are too firm, leaving them out at room temperature will help them ripen. However, if they are already at the desired ripeness, refrigeration can slow down further ripening and prolong their freshness.

3. **Ethylene Absorbers:** In a professional setting, ethylene absorbers can help control the ripening process. These products capture excess ethylene and are used to extend the shelf life of climacteric fruits during storage and transport.

4. **Separation for Preservation:** To prevent one climacteric fruit from affecting others, store them separately. For example, keep apples away from other fruits like tomatoes and bananas if you do not want them to ripen too quickly.

Handling Non-Climacteric Fruits

1. **Harvest at Peak Ripeness:** Since non-climacteric fruits do not continue to ripen after picking, they should be harvested when they are at their optimal ripeness. For instance, strawberries and grapes should be picked when they are fully ripe to ensure the best flavor.

2. **Refrigeration for Longevity:** Non-climacteric fruits often benefit from refrigeration, which can help maintain their freshness. Citrus fruits and berries should be stored in the refrigerator to extend their shelf life and preserve their quality.

3. **Avoid Ethylene Exposure:** Since these fruits do not respond to ethylene, storing them with climacteric fruits could accelerate the ripening of the climacteric fruits, which may not be desirable. Keeping non-climacteric fruits in a separate area from climacteric ones can help manage this issue.

4. **Proper Storage Conditions:** Each non-climacteric fruit has its ideal storage conditions. For instance, cherries should be stored in a cool place and consumed relatively quickly, while pineapples should be kept at room temperature if you plan to eat them soon or in the refrigerator if you need to extend their freshness.

3 Mastering Ripening Through Strategic Fruit Pairing Introduction

Ripening is more than just a natural process; it's an art form that can be enhanced through strategic practices. One of the most effective techniques to control and accelerate the ripening of fruits involves pairing them thoughtfully. Understanding how different fruits interact with each other can help you achieve perfectly ripe fruits at the right time, maximizing flavor and texture. This chapter explores the best fruit combinations for faster ripening, which pairings to avoid to prevent over-ripening, and how to balance ripening times through careful fruit pairing.

The Best Fruit Combinations for Faster Ripening

Bananas and Apples: A Classic Duo

Bananas and Apples are a powerhouse pairing when it comes to accelerating the ripening process. Both fruits are climacteric, meaning they produce ethylene gas, which is essential for ripening.

- **Ethylene Emission:** Bananas are particularly high producers of ethylene. Placing a banana near other fruits, especially apples, can significantly speed up the ripening process of the latter. Apples also emit ethylene, but at lower levels compared to bananas.
- **Practical Application:** If you have apples that are not quite ripe yet, placing them in a paper bag with a banana will help concentrate the ethylene gas, speeding up their ripening. This method is particularly useful if you want to enjoy your apples sooner.

Avocados and Bananas: Speeding Up the Process

Avocados are another fruit that benefits from ethylene exposure. Combining them with bananas can expedite their ripening.

- **Ripening Mechanics:** Avocados, when placed in a paper bag with a banana, will ripen more quickly due to the increased concentration of ethylene. This is an excellent trick if you need ripe avocados for a meal but only have hard ones on hand.
- **Storage Tips:** Make sure to check the avocados daily, as they can go from perfectly ripe to overripe quickly once ethylene levels are high.

Pears and Apples: A Harmonious Pair

Pears and Apples also work well together to speed up ripening, though the process is slightly less pronounced than with bananas.

- **Ethylene Interaction:** Pears, like apples, are climacteric and produce ethylene. Pairing them with apples can help pears ripen more evenly and quickly.
- **Usage:** This combination is particularly useful if you have a batch of pears that need a bit of a push to become ripe for consumption.

Tomatoes and Bananas: Unexpected Allies

Tomatoes and **bananas** can be an unexpected yet effective pair for ripening.

- **Ripening Benefits:** Tomatoes are climacteric and benefit from the ethylene produced by bananas. Placing tomatoes in a bowl with a banana can help them ripen faster, enhancing their sweetness and flavor.
- **Considerations:** This combination works best when you need to ripen tomatoes quickly for recipes that require fully ripe tomatoes.

Fruit Pairings to Avoid to Prevent Over-Ripening

Apples and Citrus Fruits: A Poor Match

Citrus fruits, such as **oranges** and **lemons**, should generally be kept away from apples and other climacteric fruits.

- **Ethylene Sensitivity:** Citrus fruits are non-climacteric and do not respond to ethylene. When paired with ethylene-producing fruits like apples, they can inadvertently affect the ripening of those fruits, leading to potential over-ripening.
- **Practical Tip:** Store citrus fruits separately to avoid any unintended acceleration in the ripening of climacteric fruits nearby.

Grapes and Ethylene-Producing Fruits: Keep Apart

Grapes, being non-climacteric, do not benefit from ethylene exposure and are best stored away from ethylene-producing fruits.

- **Preservation:** If grapes are stored with fruits like bananas or avocados, they can spoil more quickly due to the ethylene gas, even though they themselves do not ripen further after harvesting.
- **Storage Strategy:** Keep grapes in a cool, separate area from climacteric fruits to maintain their freshness for as long as possible.

Strawberries and Ripening Agents: Avoid Excess Ethylene

Strawberries are highly sensitive to ethylene and can spoil rapidly when exposed to high levels of this gas.

- **Ripening Concerns:** When stored with ethylene-producing fruits, strawberries can deteriorate faster than desired. This is because they do not benefit from ethylene and can become mushy or moldy.
- **Storage Advice:** Store strawberries in a separate area away from climacteric fruits to preserve their texture and flavor.

Balancing Ripening Times Through Fruit Pairing

Coordinating Ripening Schedules: A Delicate Balance

Balancing the ripening times of different fruits involves understanding their individual ripening needs and the influence of ethylene.

- **Staggered Ripening:** If you have a variety of fruits that you want to ripen in stages, use ethylene-producing fruits strategically. For instance, if you want to have ripe bananas and apples at different times, store them separately to manage their ripening processes individually.
- **Controlled Environment:** Utilize controlled environments such as paper bags or sealed containers to manage the ripening process of specific fruits. By separating climacteric fruits and managing their exposure to ethylene, you can better balance ripening times.

Practical Examples for Home Use

1. **Preparation for a Meal:** If you're planning a meal that requires ripe avocados and tomatoes, place the avocados in a paper bag with a banana to speed up their ripening. Keep the tomatoes separate until the avocados are ripe, then pair them together.
2. **Fruit Bowl Management:** In a mixed fruit bowl, arrange climacteric fruits (like apples and bananas) in one section and non-climacteric

fruits (like grapes and citrus) in another. This arrangement will help manage the ripening process more effectively and prevent unwanted over-ripening.
3. **Seasonal Storage Tips:** During different seasons, adjust your fruit storage strategies based on the types of fruits you have. For example, in the summer, you might have more climacteric fruits needing quick ripening, so use ethylene-producing fruits to your advantage. In the winter, you may have fewer options, so focus on maintaining the freshness of non-climacteric fruits by proper storage.

In Conclusion

Mastering the art of fruit ripening through strategic pairing is a valuable skill for anyone looking to enjoy perfectly ripe fruits at their peak. By understanding the interactions between climacteric and non-climacteric fruits, you can enhance the ripening process, prevent over-ripening, and balance ripening times effectively. This knowledge not only improves the quality of your fruits but also enriches your culinary experiences. With these insights, you can confidently manage your fruit ripening needs, ensuring that every bite is as delicious as possible.

4 Techniques for Perfectly Ripened Fruits: Traditional Methods vs. Modern Tools

Ripening fruits to their peak of sweetness and flavor is both an art and a science. Whether you're a home cook, gardener, or food enthusiast, understanding the various methods for achieving optimal ripeness can make a significant difference in your culinary experience. This chapter explores traditional and modern techniques for fruit ripening, providing a comprehensive guide to the pros and cons of each method. By integrating both time-tested practices and cutting-edge technologies, you can master the art of fruit ripening and enjoy perfectly ripe fruits with every meal.

The Importance of Proper Fruit Ripening

Traditional Methods: Paper Bags and Ethylene-Boosting Techniques

Paper Bags: The Classic Approach

Paper bags are a traditional and straightforward method for ripening fruits. This method leverages the natural production of ethylene, a plant hormone responsible for accelerating the ripening process.

How It Works:

- **Concentration of Ethylene:** When fruits like apples, bananas, or avocados are placed in a paper bag, the confined space helps to concentrate the ethylene gas produced by the fruits themselves. This increased concentration of ethylene speeds up the ripening process.

- **Controlled Environment:** The paper bag also protects the fruit from external environmental factors like moisture and pests, which can impact ripening.

Example: If you have unripe avocados, placing them in a paper bag with a banana can significantly speed up their ripening. The banana's high ethylene production helps the avocados reach the desired softness more quickly.

Pros:

- **Simplicity:** The paper bag method is easy to use and doesn't require special equipment.

- **Cost-Effective:** Paper bags are inexpensive and widely available.
- **Effective for Certain Fruits:** Works well for fruits that produce ethylene and need a slight boost to ripen.

Cons:

- **Limited Control:** You have less control over the exact ripening conditions, such as temperature and humidity.
- **Not Suitable for All Fruits:** Some fruits may not respond well to this method or may over-ripen if left in the bag too long.

Ethylene-Boosting Techniques: Enhancing Ripening

Ethylene-boosting techniques involve using additional ethylene sources or devices to enhance the natural ripening process.

How It Works:

- **Ethylene Emitters:** Devices or products that release controlled amounts of ethylene gas can be used to speed up ripening. These emitters are often used in commercial settings but can also be used in home environments.
- **Ethylene-Absorbing Materials:** Conversely, there are materials designed to absorb excess ethylene to prevent over-ripening. These can be used in conjunction with ethylene emitters to balance the ripening process.

Example: Ethylene emitters like Ethylene Gas Generators can be placed in storage areas to control the ripening of large quantities of fruits, ensuring uniform ripening and extending shelf life.

Pros:

- **Control:** Provides better control over the ripening process and can be tailored to specific fruits and conditions.
- **Efficient for Large Quantities:** Ideal for commercial settings or when ripening large batches of fruit.

Cons:

- **Cost:** Ethylene emitters and absorbers can be expensive.
- **Complexity:** Requires more careful monitoring and adjustment compared to simple methods like paper bags.

Modern Tools and Technologies for Fruit Ripening

Controlled Atmosphere Storage: High-Tech Ripening

Controlled Atmosphere (CA) storage involves regulating the atmosphere around the fruit to control ripening.

How It Works:

- **Gas Regulation:** CA storage controls the levels of oxygen, carbon dioxide, and humidity to slow down or accelerate ripening. By adjusting these factors, the ripening process can be precisely managed.
- **Temperature Control:** CA storage often includes temperature control to complement the gas regulation, further fine-tuning the ripening process.

Example: In commercial settings, CA storage is used to keep apples fresh for extended periods. By adjusting the atmosphere, the apples can be kept at a consistent ripeness level, extending their shelf life and reducing waste.

Pros:

- **Precision:** Allows for precise control over the ripening environment.
- **Extended Shelf Life:** Reduces spoilage and extends the shelf life of fruits.

Cons:

- **Cost:** CA storage systems are expensive and typically used in large-scale operations.
- **Complexity:** Requires specialized knowledge and equipment to

manage effectively.

Ripening Chambers: Controlled Environments

Ripening chambers are specialized environments designed to optimize ripening conditions for fruits.

How It Works:

- **Temperature and Humidity Control:** These chambers allow for precise control of temperature and humidity, essential for optimal ripening. They often include features like ethylene injection systems and ventilation to manage the ripening environment.
- **Adjustable Settings:** Chambers can be adjusted based on the specific needs of different fruits.

Example: Ripening chambers are commonly used for bananas. The chamber's settings can be adjusted to ensure bananas ripen evenly, achieving the desired texture and sweetness.

Pros:

- **Customization:** Provides customizable conditions for different types of fruits.
- **Efficiency:** Enhances ripening efficiency and quality control.

Cons:

- **Cost:** High initial investment and ongoing operational costs.
- **Maintenance:** Requires regular maintenance and monitoring to ensure optimal performance.

Ethylene Scrubbers: Managing Ethylene Levels

Ethylene scrubbers are devices used to remove excess ethylene from the air, helping to control ripening.

How It Works:

- **Absorption:** Ethylene scrubbers use materials or chemicals to absorb ethylene gas, reducing its concentration and slowing down the ripening process.

- **Integration:** Often used in conjunction with other ripening techniques to balance ethylene levels.

Example: In commercial fruit storage, ethylene scrubbers are used alongside CA storage systems to fine-tune the ripening environment and prevent over-ripening.

Pros:

- **Precision:** Allows for precise control of ethylene levels.
- **Prevent Over-Ripening:** Helps to avoid premature spoilage and maintains fruit quality.

Cons:

- **Cost:** Can be expensive to purchase and maintain.
- **Complexity:** Requires proper integration with other ripening systems.

Pros and Cons of Each Method
Traditional Methods

Paper Bags:

- **Pros:** Simple, cost-effective, and effective for some fruits.
- **Cons:** Limited control, not suitable for all fruits.

Ethylene-Boosting Techniques:

- **Pros:** Provides control over ripening, efficient for large quantities.
- **Cons:** Can be costly and complex.

Modern Tools

Controlled Atmosphere Storage:

- **Pros:** Precise control, extended shelf life.

- **Cons:** High cost, complexity.

Ripening Chambers:

- **Pros:** Customizable, enhances efficiency.
- **Cons:** Expensive, requires maintenance.

Ethylene Scrubbers:

- **Pros:** Precision in ethylene management, prevents over-ripening.
- **Cons:** Costly, complex integration.

In Conclusion

The journey to perfectly ripened fruits involves understanding and utilizing a range of techniques, from traditional methods like paper bags to advanced technologies like controlled atmosphere storage. Each method has its advantages and limitations, and the choice depends on factors such as cost, scale, and the specific needs of the fruits being ripened. By integrating these methods thoughtfully, you can achieve the desired ripeness and enhance your enjoyment of fresh, flavorful fruits. Whether you're managing a small kitchen or overseeing large-scale fruit storage, mastering these techniques will ensure that your fruits are always at their best.

5 Achieving the Perfect Ripeness: Selection, Techniques, and Culinary Uses

Perfectly ripe fruits can elevate any dish, transforming everyday meals into extraordinary experiences. The journey from selecting the right fruits to mastering ripening techniques involves a blend of science, strategy, and a touch of culinary artistry. This chapter provides a comprehensive guide to selecting fruits for ripening, tips for handling tropical fruits, strategies to avoid over-ripening, and ways to use perfectly ripe fruits in delicious recipes. Whether you're a home cook, gardener, or fruit enthusiast, these insights will help you make the most of your fruits, ensuring they are always at their peak.

How to Select the Right Fruits for Ripening

Understanding Fruit Ripeness at Purchase

Selecting fruits with the potential to ripen to perfection is the first step in ensuring you enjoy them at their best. Here's how to evaluate fruits at the time of purchase:

Climacteric vs. Non-Climacteric Fruits

- **Climacteric Fruits:** These fruits continue to ripen after being harvested. Examples include bananas, apples, avocados, pears, peaches, tomatoes, and plums. When selecting climacteric fruits, you can opt for those that are slightly under-ripe, as they will continue to mature at home.
- **Non-Climacteric Fruits:** These fruits do not ripen after harvesting and should be selected at their peak ripeness. Examples include citrus fruits, grapes, cherries, and strawberries. Choose these fruits based on immediate ripeness since they will not improve after purchase.

Visual Cues for Ripeness

- **Color:** The color of a fruit can indicate its ripeness. For instance, bananas should be yellow with a few brown spots if you want them ready to eat immediately, while avocados should be dark green or almost black with a slightly bumpy texture.

- **Texture:** The feel of the fruit is crucial. Press gently with your fingers; ripe fruits should give slightly under pressure. For example, a ripe peach will feel soft to the touch, while an unripe one will be firm.
- **Aroma:** Many fruits emit a fragrant aroma when they're ripe. Pineapples, melons, and mangoes, for instance, should smell sweet at the stem end when they are ready to eat.

Seasonality and Source

- **Seasonal Fruits:** Choose fruits that are in season as they are more likely to be fresh and flavorful. Seasonal fruits are often harvested closer to their peak ripeness.
- **Local Produce:** Whenever possible, opt for locally grown fruits. They often spend less time in transit, meaning they are harvested closer to their ripening point and maintain better quality.

Selecting Fruits for Immediate Use vs. Future Ripening

When selecting fruits, consider when you plan to use them:

Immediate Use

- For fruits you plan to eat or use in recipes within a day or two, choose those that are fully ripe at the time of purchase. Look for rich color, soft texture, and strong aroma.

Future Use

- If you're buying fruits for later use, choose those that are slightly under-ripe, especially climacteric fruits. This way, they can ripen naturally at home over several days.

Staggered Use

- To enjoy fruits over a period of time, select a mix of ripeness levels. For example, buy some peaches that are fully ripe for immediate consumption and some firmer ones for later in the week.

Tips for Ripening Tropical Fruits

Tropical fruits, with their exotic flavors and textures, require special attention when it comes to ripening. Here's how to ensure these fruits reach their peak ripeness:

Bananas

Ripening Process:

- Bananas are classic climacteric fruits that ripen well at home. Store them at room temperature, away from direct sunlight, and in a well-ventilated area. To speed up ripening, place them in a paper bag with an apple or another banana.

Ripeness Indicators:

- Bananas are ripe when their skin turns bright yellow with small brown spots. They should be soft to the touch but not mushy.

Over-Ripening Tip:

- If bananas become too ripe, peel and freeze them for later use in smoothies or baking.

Mangoes

Ripening Process:

- Mangoes can be ripened at room temperature. Placing them in a paper bag will accelerate the process. Once ripe, they should be refrigerated to slow down further ripening.

Ripeness Indicators:

- A ripe mango will have a slight give when gently pressed and emit a sweet fragrance at the stem end. The color can vary depending on the variety but generally shifts from green to a yellow-orange or red hue.

Over-Ripening Tip:

- Overripe mangoes can be pureed and used in sauces, desserts, or smoothies.

Pineapples

Ripening Process:

- Unlike some other tropical fruits, pineapples do not ripen much after being harvested. Choose pineapples with bright green leaves and a sweet aroma at the base. They should be stored at room temperature if not fully ripe and moved to the refrigerator once ripe.

Ripeness Indicators:

- A ripe pineapple has a golden-yellow color from the base up, and it should be firm with a slight softness when squeezed. The leaves should easily pull out from the crown.

Over-Ripening Tip:

- Overripe pineapple can become too soft and overly sweet, but it can still be used in baking or grilling where its sweetness is an advantage.

Papayas

Ripening Process:

- Papayas ripen well at room temperature. They should be left on the counter until they change from green to yellow-orange. Placing them in a paper bag with an ethylene-producing fruit like an apple can speed up ripening.

Ripeness Indicators:

- Ripe papayas are soft to the touch, and their skin should be mostly yellow-orange. They will emit a sweet fragrance.

Over-Ripening Tip:

- Overripe papayas can be used in smoothies, as they blend well and add natural sweetness.

Avocados

Ripening Process:

- Avocados are famous for their unique ripening process. Store them at room temperature until they soften. To speed up ripening, place them in a paper bag with a banana.

Ripeness Indicators:

- Ripe avocados yield to gentle pressure and may have a slightly darker skin. The area near the stem should also give slightly when pressed.

Over-Ripening Tip:

- If avocados become too ripe, mash them with lemon juice to make guacamole, or use them in smoothies or spreads.

How to Avoid Over-ripening and Maintain Freshness

While it's important to ripen fruits to their peak, avoiding over-ripening is crucial to prevent waste and maintain quality. Here are strategies to keep your fruits fresh for as long as possible:

Proper Storage Techniques

Refrigeration:

- Once fruits reach their desired ripeness, many should be stored in the refrigerator to slow down the ripening process. This is particularly true for climacteric fruits like apples, pears, and avocados.

Freezing:

- Overripe fruits can be frozen for later use. Berries, bananas, and mangoes freeze particularly well and can be used in smoothies, baking, or desserts after thawing.

Controlled Ripening:

- For fruits that ripen unevenly, such as peaches or plums, consider storing them in a single layer at room temperature. Once they start to soften, refrigerate them to maintain their freshness.

Using Ethylene Absorbers

Ethylene Absorbers:

- Ethylene absorbers are a practical solution to control ripening, especially in storage areas where ethylene-producing fruits are kept alongside non-climacteric fruits. These devices or materials absorb excess ethylene gas, preventing over-ripening.

Staggered Ripening Strategy

Planning Consumption:

- To avoid having too many ripe fruits at once, stagger your fruit purchases and consider their ripening times. Buy a mix of fruits with different ripening speeds and store them accordingly.

Monitoring Fruit Ripeness

Regular Checks:

- Keep an eye on your fruit's ripeness daily. Remove fruits from paper bags or controlled environments as soon as they reach the desired ripeness, and move them to the refrigerator if you're not ready to use them immediately.

Recipes and Uses for Perfectly Ripe Fruits

Now that you have mastered the art of ripening fruits, it's time to enjoy them in a variety of delicious ways. Here are some recipes and ideas for using perfectly ripe fruits:

Banana Bread with Overripe Bananas

Ingredients:

- 3-4 overripe bananas, mashed
- 1/3 cup melted butter
- 1 teaspoon baking soda
- Pinch of salt
- 3/4 cup sugar
- 1 large egg, beaten
- 1 teaspoon vanilla extract
- 1 1/2 cups all-purpose flour

Instructions:

1. Preheat your oven to 350°F (175°C), and grease a 4x8 inch loaf pan.
2. In a mixing bowl, mash the ripe bananas with a fork until smooth. Stir the melted butter into the mashed bananas.
3. Mix in the baking soda and salt. Stir in the sugar, beaten egg, and vanilla extract. Mix in the flour.
4. Pour the batter into your prepared loaf pan.
5. Bake for 60 minutes, or until a toothpick inserted into the center comes out clean.
6. Let cool before removing from the pan. Slice and enjoy!

Avocado and Mango Salad

Ingredients:

- 2 ripe avocados, diced
- 1 ripe mango, peeled and diced
- 1/2 red onion, finely chopped
- 1 red bell pepper, diced
- 1/4 cup chopped cilantro
- Juice of 1 lime
- Salt and pepper to taste

Instructions:

1. In a large bowl, combine the diced avocado, mango, red onion, red bell pepper, and cilantro.
2. Drizzle with lime juice, and season with salt and pepper.

3. Gently toss the salad to mix all ingredients without mashing the avocado.
4. Serve immediately as a refreshing side dish or with grilled chicken or fish.

Grilled Pineapple with Honey and Cinnamon

Ingredients:

- 1 ripe pineapple, peeled, cored, and sliced into rings
- 2 tablespoons honey
- 1 teaspoon ground cinnamon

Instructions:

1. Preheat your grill to medium heat.
2. In a small bowl, mix the honey and cinnamon.
3. Brush each pineapple ring with the honey-cinnamon mixture.
4. Place the pineapple rings on the grill, and cook for 3-4 minutes per side, until grill marks appear and the pineapple is heated through.
5. Remove from the grill and serve warm as a dessert or side dish.

Mango Smoothie Bowl

Ingredients:

- 1 ripe mango, peeled and chopped
- 1 frozen banana
- 1/2 cup Greek yogurt
- 1/2 cup orange juice
- Toppings: fresh berries, granola, chia seeds, coconut flakes

Instructions:

1. In a blender, combine the mango, frozen banana, Greek yogurt, and orange juice. Blend until smooth.
2. Pour the smoothie into a bowl.
3. Top with fresh berries, granola, chia seeds, and coconut flakes as desired.
4. Serve immediately as a nutritious breakfast or snack.

Avocado Chocolate Mousse

The Art Of Ripening Fruits

Ingredients:

- 2 ripe avocados
- 1/4 cup unsweetened cocoa powder
- 1/4 cup honey or maple syrup
- 1/2 teaspoon vanilla extract
- Pinch of salt
- Optional toppings: whipped cream, berries, chocolate shavings

Instructions:

1. Scoop the avocado flesh into a food processor or blender.
2. Add the cocoa powder, honey or maple syrup, vanilla extract, and salt.
3. Blend until smooth and creamy.
4. Taste and adjust sweetness as needed.
5. Spoon the mousse into serving dishes and chill in the refrigerator for at least 30 minutes before serving.
6. Top with whipped cream, berries, or chocolate shavings if desired.

Pineapple Upside-Down Cake

Ingredients:

- 1/4 cup butter, melted
- 1/2 cup packed brown sugar
- 1 ripe pineapple, sliced into rings
- Maraschino cherries (optional)
- 1 1/2 cups all-purpose flour
- 1 cup granulated sugar
- 1/2 cup unsalted butter, softened
- 2 large eggs
- 2 teaspoons baking powder
- 1/4 teaspoon salt
- 1/2 cup milk
- 1 teaspoon vanilla extract

Instructions:

1. Preheat your oven to 350°F (175°C). Grease a 9-inch round cake pan.
2. Pour the melted butter into the prepared pan, and sprinkle the brown sugar evenly over the butter.

3. Arrange the pineapple slices over the sugar mixture, and place a cherry in the center of each pineapple ring if using.
4. In a large bowl, beat the flour, granulated sugar, softened butter, eggs, baking powder, salt, milk, and vanilla extract until smooth.
5. Pour the batter over the pineapple slices in the pan.
6. Bake for 45-50 minutes, or until a toothpick inserted into the center comes out clean.
7. Let the cake cool for 5 minutes in the pan, then invert it onto a serving plate.
8. Serve warm or at room temperature, topped with whipped cream if desired.

In Conclusion

The process of selecting, ripening, and utilizing fruits is an essential skill for anyone who appreciates fresh produce. By understanding the characteristics of different fruits and applying the appropriate ripening techniques, you can ensure that your fruits reach their peak flavor and texture. Whether you're enjoying them fresh, incorporating them into recipes, or preserving them for later use, perfectly ripened fruits will enhance your culinary creations and bring a burst of natural sweetness to your table. As you continue to explore the art of ripening fruits, you'll discover new ways to make the most of every piece of fruit you bring into your kitchen.

6 Mastering the Storage and Preservation of Ripe Fruits

The journey of fruit from the tree to your table doesn't end with ripening. To truly enjoy the flavors and nutritional benefits that ripe fruits offer, it's essential to know how to store and preserve them correctly. Proper storage techniques can extend the shelf life of fruits, while preservation methods like freezing can allow you to enjoy seasonal fruits year-round. This chapter will explore best practices for storing ripe fruits, techniques to maintain their freshness, and methods for freezing fruits to enjoy them later. Whether you're a home cook, gardener, or food enthusiast, mastering these skills will help you make the most of your fruits.

Best Practices for Storing Ripe Fruits

Storing ripe fruits properly is crucial for maintaining their taste, texture, and nutritional value. Different fruits have different storage needs, and understanding these can help you prevent spoilage and waste.

Understanding the Basics of Fruit Storage
Temperature Matters:

- **Refrigeration:** Most ripe fruits should be stored in the refrigerator to slow down the ripening process. The cool temperature reduces the activity of enzymes that cause fruits to continue ripening and eventually spoil.
- **Room Temperature:** Some fruits, such as bananas, avocados, and tomatoes, should be stored at room temperature, even when ripe. Refrigeration can alter their texture and flavor, making them less enjoyable.

Humidity Control:

- **High Humidity:** Fruits like berries, grapes, and citrus fruits benefit from high humidity environments. Storing them in the crisper drawer of your refrigerator helps maintain their moisture and prevent them from drying out.
- **Low Humidity:** Fruits like onions and garlic should be stored in a low-humidity environment to prevent mold growth. A cool, dry place like a pantry or cellar is ideal.

Ethylene Sensitivity:

- **Ethylene-Producing Fruits:** Some fruits, such as apples, bananas, and avocados, produce ethylene gas, which accelerates ripening. These should be stored away from ethylene-sensitive fruits like berries and leafy greens to prevent premature spoilage.
- **Ethylene Absorbers:** Consider using ethylene absorbers or placing ethylene-producing fruits in separate bags or containers to extend the freshness of other produce.

Storing Specific Types of Ripe Fruits

Apples:

- **Refrigeration:** Store apples in the crisper drawer of your refrigerator. They can last for several weeks to months if kept at a temperature just above freezing. To prevent bruising, store them in a single layer or in a padded container.

Bananas:

- **Room Temperature:** Bananas should be stored at room temperature, even when ripe. If you want to slow down ripening, you can refrigerate them, but the peel will darken. The fruit inside will remain fresh and edible.

Berries:

- **Refrigeration:** Berries are highly perishable and should be refrigerated immediately. Store them in a single layer on a paper towel inside a container to absorb excess moisture. Do not wash berries until you are ready to eat them, as moisture can cause them to spoil more quickly.

Citrus Fruits:

- **Room Temperature:** Citrus fruits can be stored at room temperature for up to a week. If you need to keep them longer, store them in the refrigerator, where they can last several weeks. Keep them in a mesh bag or a container that allows air circulation.

Avocados:

- **Ripen First:** Avocados should be ripened at room temperature. Once they reach the desired ripeness, move them to the refrigerator to keep them fresh for a few more days. If you've cut an avocado, sprinkle the exposed flesh with lemon juice, cover it tightly with plastic wrap, and refrigerate it to prevent browning.

Stone Fruits (Peaches, Plums, Nectarines):

- **Refrigeration:** Stone fruits should be refrigerated once they are ripe. Store them in a single layer to prevent bruising, which can lead to quicker spoilage. They can last up to a week in the refrigerator.

Grapes:

- **Refrigeration:** Grapes should be refrigerated immediately after purchase. Keep them in their original packaging or a breathable container to allow air circulation. Avoid washing grapes until you are ready to eat them to prevent moisture buildup and mold growth.

Mangoes and Pineapples:

- **Ripen First:** Mangoes and pineapples should be ripened at room temperature. Once ripe, move them to the refrigerator to keep them fresh. Pineapples should be stored whole in the refrigerator to preserve their flavor.

Melons:

- **Whole vs. Cut:** Whole melons should be stored at room temperature until ripe. Once cut, store them in the refrigerator. Cover the cut surfaces with plastic wrap to prevent them from drying out.

Using Proper Containers for Storage

Plastic Bags and Containers:

- **Sealable Bags:** Resealable plastic bags can help maintain humidity for fruits like apples and grapes. Ensure the bags are not sealed too tightly to allow for some air circulation.
- **Plastic Containers:** These are ideal for storing more delicate fruits like berries. They protect the fruits from getting crushed and help maintain moisture levels.

Glass Containers:

- **Airtight Glass Jars:** Glass containers are excellent for storing cut fruits, such as apples or avocados. They help prevent flavor transfer and keep fruits fresh without the risk of chemicals leaching into the food.

Paper Bags:

- **Ethylene Management:** Paper bags are useful for ripening fruits that emit ethylene gas, such as avocados and bananas. The paper allows the fruit to breathe while trapping enough ethylene to promote even ripening.

Ventilated Baskets:

- **Room Temperature Storage:** Ventilated baskets are perfect for storing fruits at room temperature, such as bananas and citrus fruits. They provide adequate air circulation, preventing moisture buildup that can lead to spoilage.

Techniques to Preserve Freshness

Even with proper storage, ripe fruits have a limited shelf life. To extend their freshness, various techniques can be employed, ensuring your fruits remain tasty and nutritious for as long as possible.

Acidic Solutions to Prevent Oxidation

Lemon or Lime Juice:

- **Preventing Browning:** Fruits like apples, pears, and avocados tend to brown quickly when exposed to air. Brushing or sprinkling them with lemon or lime juice can prevent this oxidation, preserving their appearance and flavor.

Vinegar Solutions:

- **Mold Prevention:** A solution of water and vinegar can be used to soak fruits like berries. This kills mold spores and extends their freshness. After soaking, rinse the berries and dry them thoroughly before storing.

Salad Freshness:

- **Citrus-Based Dressings:** When preparing fruit salads, using a citrus-based dressing helps preserve the colors and flavors of the fruits by slowing down the enzymatic browning process.

Dehydration for Long-Term Preservation

Dried Fruits:

- **Making Dried Fruits at Home:** Dehydrating fruits like apples, apricots, and mangoes is an excellent way to preserve their freshness and flavor for months. You can use a dehydrator or a low-temperature oven for this process. Dehydrated fruits are perfect for snacking or adding to cereals and trail mixes.

Storing Dried Fruits:

- **Airtight Storage:** Once dried, store fruits in airtight containers in a cool, dark place. Properly dried and stored fruits can last for several months and provide a nutritious, shelf-stable snack.

Benefits of Dehydration:

- **Nutrient Concentration:** Dehydration preserves most of the nutrients in fruits while concentrating their natural sugars, making them a healthy alternative to sugary snacks.
- **Portability:** Dried fruits are lightweight, portable, and do not require refrigeration, making them ideal for travel and outdoor activities.

Fermentation for Extended Shelf Life

Fruit Fermentation:

- **Traditional Preservation:** Fermenting fruits is a traditional method of preservation that not only extends the shelf life but also enhances the nutritional value. Fermented fruits can be used in various recipes, adding a tangy, probiotic-rich element to your diet.

Making Fermented Fruit Preserves:

- **Versatile Use:** Fermented fruits can be used in sauces, condiments, or as a side dish. They add a unique flavor to meals and are a staple in many traditional cuisines.

Storing Fermented Fruits:

- **Refrigeration:** Fermented fruits should be stored in the refrigerator, where they can last for several months. The cool temperature slows down the fermentation process, preventing the fruits from becoming overly sour.

Sugaring and Salting for Preservation

Candied Fruits:

- **Sugaring Method:** Sugaring is a preservation method where fruits are coated in sugar and cooked to create candied fruits. These can be stored for extended periods and used in baking or as a sweet treat.

Syrup Preservation:

- **Preserving in Syrup:** Fruits like peaches or cherries can be preserved in a sugar syrup, extending their shelf life and retaining their flavor. Store these preserved fruits in sterilized jars in a cool, dark place.

Salt-Preserved Fruits:

- **Preserving with Salt:** Salt can be used to preserve fruits like lemons, turning them into tangy condiments that add flavor to a variety of dishes. Salt draws out moisture, creating an environment that inhibits bacterial growth.

Shelf Life Extension:

- **Long-Term Storage:** Salt-preserved fruits can last for several months to a year when stored in a cool, dry place. They add a unique flavor to dishes and are a traditional preservation method in many cultures.

How to Freeze Ripe Fruits for Later Use

Freezing is one of the most effective ways to preserve ripe fruits for later use. It allows you to enjoy the taste of seasonal fruits year-round and reduces waste by preserving fruits that might otherwise spoil.

Preparing Fruits for Freezing

Washing and Drying:

- **Clean and Dry:** Before freezing fruits, wash them thoroughly to remove any dirt, pesticides, or bacteria. Dry them completely, as excess moisture can lead to ice crystals forming on the fruit, affecting their texture.

Cutting and Prepping:

- **Pre-Cut for Convenience:** Cut fruits into the desired size before freezing. This makes it easier to use them directly from the freezer for smoothies, baking, or snacking.
- **Blanching:** For some fruits, such as peaches and apples, blanching (briefly boiling and then cooling them) can help preserve their color, flavor, and texture during freezing.

Using Acid to Prevent Browning:

- **Lemon or Ascorbic Acid:** Toss cut fruits like apples, pears, and peaches in lemon juice or a solution of ascorbic acid before freezing. This prevents browning and maintains their bright color.

Methods for Freezing Fruits

Flash Freezing:

- **Single-Layer Freeze:** Spread the prepared fruit pieces in a single layer on a baking sheet and freeze until solid. This prevents the pieces from sticking together, making it easier to store them in bulk later.

Freezing in Syrup:

- **Syrup Pack Method:** For fruits that tend to become mushy when frozen, such as berries or peaches, freezing them in a sugar syrup can help preserve their texture. Place the fruits in containers, cover them with syrup, and freeze.

Dry Pack Freezing:

- **Bagging Method:** Once fruits are flash-frozen, transfer them to airtight freezer bags. Remove as much air as possible to prevent freezer burn, which can degrade the quality of the fruit.

Best Practices for Storing Frozen Fruits

Labeling and Organization:

- **Label Containers:** Always label your containers with the type of fruit and the date they were frozen. This helps you keep track of freshness and ensures you use older fruits first.
- **Organize by Type:** Store fruits in the freezer in an organized manner, grouping similar types together. This makes it easier to find what you need without leaving the freezer open for too long, which can cause temperature fluctuations.

Optimal Freezing Temperatures:

- **Deep Freezing:** The ideal temperature for storing frozen fruits is 0°F (-18°C) or lower. At this temperature, fruits can be stored for up to a year without significant loss of quality.

Thawing Frozen Fruits:

- **Slow Thawing:** To maintain the best texture and flavor, thaw frozen fruits slowly in the refrigerator. Avoid using the microwave, as it can cause uneven thawing and make the fruits mushy.
- **Using Frozen Fruits:** Frozen fruits are perfect for smoothies, baking, and cooking. You can also enjoy them as a refreshing snack on a hot day, straight from the freezer.

Conclusion

Storing and preserving ripe fruits is an art that requires a blend of knowledge and technique. By following the best practices for storage, utilizing various preservation techniques, and learning how to freeze fruits effectively, you can extend the life of your fruits and enjoy them in various forms throughout the year. Whether you're savoring a perfectly ripe peach in the middle of winter or adding a handful of frozen berries to your morning smoothie, these strategies will help you make the most of nature's bounty. With a little care and attention, you can ensure that your fruits remain as fresh, flavorful, and nutritious as the day they were picked.

7 Navigating the World of Ripening: Myths, FAQs, and Common Mistakes

Fruit ripening is both an art and a science, steeped in tradition and backed by modern research. Yet, the journey from unripe to perfectly ripe can be clouded by misconceptions and misunderstandings. This chapter aims to clear the fog surrounding fruit ripening by debunking popular myths, addressing frequently asked questions, and highlighting common mistakes and how to avoid them. Whether you're a home cook looking to enhance your fruit experience or a gardener seeking to perfect your produce, understanding these aspects will empower you to achieve optimal ripeness and flavor.

Debunking Popular Myths About Ripening

Fruit ripening is often surrounded by myths that can lead to confusion and improper handling. Let's separate fact from fiction to help you get the most out of your fruits.

Myth 1: "All Fruits Ripen the Same Way"

Reality: Fruits ripen differently based on their type and natural ripening process. Climacteric fruits, such as bananas, apples, and avocados, continue to ripen after being picked due to the production of ethylene gas. Non-climacteric fruits, such as berries and grapes, stop ripening once harvested. Understanding these differences is crucial for proper storage and ripening techniques.

Example: A banana will continue to ripen and soften at room temperature, while a strawberry will not improve in ripeness after being picked.

Myth 2: "Putting Fruits in a Brown Paper Bag Always Ripens Them Faster"

Reality: While a brown paper bag can speed up ripening for some fruits by trapping ethylene gas, it's not a universal solution. The effectiveness of this method depends on the type of fruit and its ripeness stage. For some fruits, like avocados and bananas, this method works well, but for others, it might not make a significant difference.

Example: Apples and pears ripen well in a paper bag due to their ethylene production, but berries, which are sensitive to moisture, can become mushy if placed in a paper bag.

Myth 3: "Ripening Fruits in the Sun is Always Beneficial"

Reality: Direct sunlight can actually cause some fruits to ripen unevenly or deteriorate faster due to heat. While sunlight can aid in the ripening of some fruits like tomatoes, many fruits, including apples and peaches, are better off ripening in a cool, shaded area.

Example: Tomatoes benefit from sunlight, but placing peaches in direct sunlight can lead to a sunburn effect, affecting their taste and texture.

Myth 4: "Refrigeration Stops Ripening Completely"

Reality: Refrigeration slows down the ripening process but doesn't stop it entirely. Some fruits, like apples and pears, will continue to ripen, albeit more slowly, when stored in the refrigerator. Others, such as bananas and avocados, should not be refrigerated until they are ripe to avoid altering their texture and flavor.

Example: A ripe apple will stay fresh longer in the refrigerator, but an unripe avocado will not develop its creamy texture if placed in the fridge too soon.

Myth 5: "Ethylene Gas is Harmful to Fruits"

Reality: Ethylene gas is a natural ripening hormone produced by many fruits. While it can cause fruits to ripen faster, it is not harmful in moderate amounts. In fact, ethylene gas is used in controlled environments to ripen fruits in commercial settings.

Example: Ethylene-producing fruits like bananas and apples can be used to speed up the ripening of avocados by placing them in a closed paper bag together.

Frequently Asked Questions About Fruit Ripening

1. How can I tell if a fruit is ripe without tasting it?

Answer: The ripeness of a fruit can often be assessed by its color, firmness, and aroma. For example:

- **Avocados:** Ripe avocados yield to gentle pressure but are not mushy. They also have a darker skin color.
- **Peaches:** Ripe peaches are fragrant and slightly soft to the touch.
- **Tomatoes:** Ripe tomatoes have a rich color and are slightly firm, but not hard.

2. What's the best way to ripen fruits faster?

Answer: To ripen fruits faster, you can use ethylene-producing fruits like apples or bananas to help. Place the fruit in a paper bag with one of these ripeners. The confined space allows ethylene gas to build up, accelerating the ripening process. Alternatively, placing fruits in a warm, sunny spot can also speed up ripening for certain types of fruit.

3. Can I store unripe fruits with ripe ones?

Answer: It's generally not advisable to store unripe and ripe fruits together, especially if the ripe fruits are ethylene producers. The ethylene gas released by ripe fruits can cause the unripe ones to ripen too quickly and unevenly. It's best to separate them to control the ripening process more effectively.

4. How can I prevent over-ripening of fruits?

Answer: To prevent over-ripening:

- **Monitor Regularly:** Check fruits frequently to ensure they don't over-ripen.
- **Use Refrigeration:** For fruits that are prone to fast ripening, refrigeration can slow the process once they reach the desired ripeness.
- **Proper Storage:** Store fruits in appropriate conditions based on their ripening needs. For instance, keep ethylene-sensitive fruits away from ethylene-producing ones.

5. What's the best way to handle fruits that are already overripe?

Answer: Overripe fruits can still be used creatively. Consider:

- **Baking:** Overripe bananas can be used in banana bread or muffins.
- **Smoothies:** Overripe fruits are perfect for smoothies or fruit sauces.
- **Preservation:** Overripe fruits can be preserved through canning or making jams and compotes.

Common Mistakes and How to Avoid Them

Mistake 1: Not Understanding Fruit Types

Issue: Assuming all fruits ripen the same way can lead to improper handling and storage.

Solution: Learn the specific ripening processes for different fruits. For example, know that climacteric fruits like apples continue ripening after picking, while non-climacteric fruits like strawberries do not.

Mistake 2: Improper Storage Methods

Issue: Using incorrect storage methods can lead to faster spoilage or poor ripening.

Solution: Store fruits according to their needs:

- **Climacteric Fruits:** Room temperature for ripening, then refrigerate.
- **Non-Climacteric Fruits:** Refrigeration from the start to maintain freshness.

Mistake 3: Over-Relying on Ripening Tricks

Issue: Relying solely on methods like paper bags or placing fruits near ethylene producers can be ineffective or even detrimental.

Solution: Use ripening tricks as part of a broader strategy. Combine them with proper storage and handling techniques to achieve the best results.

Mistake 4: Ignoring Ripeness Indicators

Issue: Not checking fruits regularly can lead to over-ripening or spoilage.

Solution: Regularly inspect fruits for signs of ripeness such as color changes, firmness, and aroma. Adjust your storage methods as needed based on these observations.

Mistake 5: Mismanaging Ethylene Production

Issue: Not accounting for ethylene gas production can cause some fruits to ripen too quickly or spoil prematurely.

Solution: Separate ethylene-producing fruits from those sensitive to ethylene. Use ethylene absorbers if needed to manage ripening effectively.

Conclusion

Navigating the complexities of fruit ripening involves debunking myths, understanding frequently asked questions, and avoiding common mistakes. By being informed about the true nature of ripening, you can make better decisions about how to handle and store your fruits. Armed with this knowledge, you'll be able to achieve perfectly ripe fruits every time, enhancing your culinary experiences and reducing waste. Whether you're striving to perfect your home fruit storage or simply looking to enjoy the freshest flavors, these insights will guide you toward success in the art of fruit ripening.

8. Mastering the Art of Seasonal Fruit Ripening

The quest for perfectly ripe fruit is a journey that varies with the seasons. Each time of year brings its own unique set of fruits, each requiring different strategies for optimal ripening and freshness. Whether you're basking in the heat of summer, enjoying the crispness of autumn, enduring the chill of winter, or anticipating the first signs of spring, understanding how to manage and enjoy seasonal fruits will elevate your culinary experience and reduce food waste. This chapter delves into the best practices for ripening and storing fruits throughout the year, providing practical tips and insights tailored to each season.

Summer Fruits: How to Combine for Optimal Ripening

Summer is a season of abundance, with a variety of fruits reaching their peak ripeness. To make the most of this bountiful time, it's essential to understand how to handle summer fruits for optimal ripening and flavor.

Key Summer Fruits and Ripening Techniques

1. Peaches and Nectarines

- **Combining for Ripeness:** These stone fruits benefit from ethylene-producing fruits like apples and bananas. Place peaches and nectarines in a paper bag with one of these fruits to speed up ripening.
- **Storage Tips:** Once ripe, store them in the refrigerator to prevent over-ripening. They should be consumed within a few days to enjoy their best flavor and texture.

2. Berries (Strawberries, Blueberries, Raspberries)

- **Ripening Insights:** Berries are generally harvested when they are ripe. However, they can continue to ripen slightly if left at room temperature. Be cautious, as they spoil quickly.
- **Storage Tips:** Store berries in the refrigerator in a breathable container to prevent mold. Wash them only before consumption to extend their shelf life.

3. Melons (Cantaloupe, Honeydew, Watermelon)

- **Combining for Ripeness:** Melons generally ripen on the vine and don't continue to ripen much after picking. However, placing a ripe melon near ethylene-producing fruits can slightly enhance flavor if the melon is near ripe.
- **Storage Tips:** Store melons at room temperature if they are not fully ripe. Once ripe, refrigerate to maintain freshness, but consume them promptly.

Seasonal Tips for Optimal Ripening

- **Monitor Temperature:** Summer heat can accelerate ripening. Check fruits daily to avoid over-ripening.
- **Use Paper Bags:** For fruits that continue to ripen, use paper bags to control ethylene exposure and speed up the process effectively.

Autumn Fruits: Tips for Long-Term Freshness

Autumn brings a shift from the juicy, delicate fruits of summer to hardier, more storage-friendly options. Proper handling and storage techniques are crucial to extend the shelf life of these fruits and enjoy them throughout the season.

Key Autumn Fruits and Storage Strategies

1. Apples

- **Ripening and Storage:** Apples are climacteric fruits and continue to ripen after harvesting. Store them in a cool, dark place or in the refrigerator to maintain their crispness. Apples can be stored for several months if kept in optimal conditions.
- **Long-Term Storage:** For long-term storage, keep apples in a crisper drawer or an airtight container to prevent moisture loss and flavor degradation.

2. Pears

- **Ripening Techniques:** Pears ripen off the tree and should be kept at room temperature until they yield slightly to pressure near the stem. Once ripe, refrigerate them to extend freshness.
- **Preservation Tips:** Pears can be preserved by canning or making pear sauce, which is ideal for enjoying them beyond their peak season.

3. Pomegranates

- **Ripening Insights:** Pomegranates are harvested when ripe and do not ripen further after picking. Store them in a cool, dry place or in the refrigerator.
- **Storage Tips:** Pomegranates can last for several weeks in the fridge. For longer storage, you can freeze the arils (seeds) for use in recipes or snacks.

Seasonal Tips for Long-Term Freshness

- **Regular Inspection:** Check stored fruits regularly for any signs of spoilage or overripening.
- **Optimal Conditions:** Maintain a cool and consistent temperature for autumn fruits to preserve their quality over time.

Winter Fruits: Ripening Techniques for Cold Weather

Winter's cold weather presents unique challenges for ripening fruits, as many are not at their peak during this season. Proper techniques can help maximize flavor and texture despite the chilly temperatures.

Key Winter Fruits and Ripening Techniques

1. Citrus Fruits (Oranges, Grapefruits, Lemons)

- **Ripening and Storage:** Citrus fruits are typically harvested when ripe. They should be kept in a cool, dry place or in the refrigerator. Citrus fruits can last for several weeks to months when stored properly.
- **Flavor Enhancement:** To enhance flavor, keep citrus fruits at room temperature for a few days before consuming.

2. Kiwi

- **Ripening Insights:** Kiwi is a climacteric fruit and can be ripened at room temperature. Place kiwis in a paper bag with an apple to speed up the process.
- **Storage Tips:** Once ripe, refrigerate kiwis to extend their shelf life. They are best consumed within a week of ripening.

3. Pomegranates (continued)

- **Winter Use:** Pomegranates are excellent winter fruits due to their longevity in storage. They provide a burst of flavor and nutrition during the colder months.

Seasonal Tips for Cold Weather Ripening

- **Room Temperature:** For fruits that need to ripen, keep them at room temperature away from drafts and direct sunlight.
- **Monitor Humidity:** Winter air can be dry, so consider using a humidifier in the storage area to prevent fruits from drying out.

Spring Fruits: Preparing for Seasonal Bounty

Spring heralds the arrival of fresh, new fruits, and proper preparation can help you enjoy the seasonal bounty to the fullest. As you transition from winter to spring, understanding how to handle these new arrivals is key.

Key Spring Fruits and Preparation Tips

1. Strawberries

- **Seasonal Arrival:** Strawberries begin to peak in early spring. They are often sweeter and more flavorful when picked fresh.
- **Preparation Tips:** Store strawberries in the refrigerator and wash them only before eating to prevent spoilage. Enjoy them fresh or use them in recipes like jams and desserts.

2. Rhubarb

- **Handling and Storage:** Rhubarb is often used in pies and crumbles. Store rhubarb in the refrigerator and use it within a week for the best flavor.
- **Preparation Tips:** Rhubarb should be cooked before consumption. Combine it with strawberries for a classic spring dessert.

3. Cherries

- **Ripening Insights:** Cherries are best when they are fully ripe. Store them in the refrigerator and consume them within a week to enjoy their peak flavor.

- **Preservation Tips:** For long-term use, cherries can be frozen. Flash-freezing them on a baking sheet before transferring them to freezer bags will help preserve their quality.

Seasonal Tips for Spring Preparation

- **Early Harvests:** Be aware that early spring fruits might not be at their peak. Use them in recipes that enhance their flavors, such as jams and baked goods.
- **Storage Transition:** As you prepare for the influx of spring fruits, consider adjusting your storage methods to accommodate the new variety and volume.

Conclusion

Understanding and managing the ripening of fruits across different seasons can significantly enhance your enjoyment of seasonal produce. By applying the right techniques for each type of fruit and each season, you can maximize flavor, extend freshness, and reduce waste. From the summer's juicy peaches to winter's hearty citrus, mastering these seasonal ripening strategies ensures that you'll always have the perfect fruit at your fingertips. Embrace the rhythms of the seasons and let your fruit ripening journey be a delightful exploration of taste and texture year-round.

9. Celebrating Ripe Fruits: Creative Uses and Delicious Recipes

Once you've perfected the art of ripening fruits, the next step is to revel in their peak flavors and textures. This chapter explores the exciting ways to use ripe fruits in your kitchen, from refreshing smoothies and indulgent desserts to preserving techniques for future enjoyment. We'll also delve into creative presentation ideas to make your fruit-based dishes as visually appealing as they are delicious. Whether you're a home cook eager to experiment with ripe fruit recipes or a gardener looking to make the most of your harvest, this chapter provides a bounty of ideas to enhance your culinary repertoire.

Smoothies and Natural Juices

Smoothies and natural juices are perhaps the simplest and most satisfying ways to enjoy ripe fruits. They offer a versatile canvas for combining different flavors and nutrients while showcasing the natural sweetness and freshness of ripe produce.

Classic Fruit Smoothies

1. Berry Bliss Smoothie

- **Ingredients:** Ripe strawberries, blueberries, and raspberries. Add a banana for creaminess and a splash of orange juice for a tangy twist.
- **Instructions:** Blend the berries with a banana and a splash of orange juice until smooth. For a thicker consistency, add a handful of ice cubes or Greek yogurt.

2. Tropical Dream Smoothie

- **Ingredients:** Ripe mango, pineapple, and banana. Add a dash of coconut water for a tropical flair.
- **Instructions:** Combine chopped mango, pineapple, and banana in a blender with a splash of coconut water. Blend until creamy, adding more coconut water if needed for the desired consistency.

3. Green Power Smoothie

- **Ingredients:** Ripe kiwi, apple, and a handful of spinach. Add a squeeze of lime juice for brightness.

- **Instructions:** Blend the kiwi, apple, and spinach with a splash of water or coconut water. For added sweetness, include a tablespoon of honey or agave syrup.

Natural Juices

1. Refreshing Citrus Juice

- **Ingredients:** Ripe oranges, grapefruits, and a lemon.
- **Instructions:** Juice the oranges, grapefruits, and lemon. Serve chilled over ice for a refreshing, vitamin C-packed beverage.

2. Apple and Pear Juice

- **Ingredients:** Ripe apples and pears.
- **Instructions:** Juice the apples and pears together for a sweet, naturally flavored juice. Serve immediately to enjoy the fresh taste.

3. Melon Medley Juice

- **Ingredients:** Ripe cantaloupe and honeydew melon.
- **Instructions:** Blend the melons until smooth, then strain through a fine mesh sieve to remove pulp. Serve chilled, garnished with mint leaves.

Tips for Perfect Smoothies and Juices

- **Use Frozen Fruit:** For a colder, thicker smoothie, use frozen fruit or add ice cubes to the blender.
- **Balance Flavors:** Adjust sweetness and acidity by experimenting with different fruit combinations and adding a splash of citrus or a drizzle of honey.
- **Nutrient Boosts:** Enhance your smoothies with additional nutrients by adding a handful of spinach, chia seeds, or protein powder.

Desserts Featuring Ripe Fruits

Ripe fruits are the stars of many delightful desserts, offering natural sweetness and vibrant flavors that can elevate even the simplest recipes. Here are some delectable ways to use ripe fruits in your desserts.

Fruit Tarts and Pies

The Art Of Ripening Fruits

1. Fresh Berry Tart

- **Ingredients:** Ripe strawberries, blueberries, raspberries, and a tart shell. Use a creamy filling made from mascarpone cheese and vanilla.
- **Instructions:** Pre-bake the tart shell, then fill with a mixture of mascarpone cheese, vanilla, and a touch of honey. Top with a colorful assortment of fresh berries.

2. Classic Apple Pie

- **Ingredients:** Ripe apples, cinnamon, nutmeg, and a pie crust.
- **Instructions:** Toss sliced apples with cinnamon and nutmeg, then fill a pie crust and top with another layer of crust or a crumble topping. Bake until the apples are tender and the crust is golden.

3. Peach Cobbler

- **Ingredients:** Ripe peaches, sugar, flour, and butter. Add a hint of vanilla and a dash of cinnamon.
- **Instructions:** Toss sliced peaches with sugar and a bit of flour. Place in a baking dish and top with a mixture of flour, sugar, and butter. Bake until bubbly and golden.

Fruit-Based Cakes and Muffins

1. Banana Bread

- **Ingredients:** Ripe bananas, flour, sugar, and baking soda.
- **Instructions:** Mash the ripe bananas and mix with flour, sugar, and baking soda. Bake in a loaf pan until a toothpick comes out clean.

2. Blueberry Muffins

- **Ingredients:** Ripe blueberries, flour, sugar, and baking powder.
- **Instructions:** Gently fold fresh blueberries into a muffin batter made with flour, sugar, and baking powder. Bake until golden brown and a toothpick comes out clean.

3. Pineapple Upside-Down Cake

- **Ingredients:** Ripe pineapple rings, brown sugar, butter, and cake batter.

- **Instructions:** Arrange pineapple rings in a pan with brown sugar and butter. Pour cake batter over the top and bake until golden. Invert to reveal a caramelized pineapple topping.

Tips for Fruit Desserts

- **Choose Ripe Fruit:** The best desserts start with perfectly ripe fruit. Avoid overripe or underripe fruit, which can affect texture and flavor.
- **Incorporate Spices:** Enhance the natural flavors of fruit with complementary spices like cinnamon, nutmeg, and vanilla.
- **Serve Fresh:** Many fruit-based desserts taste best when served fresh. Consider making desserts shortly before serving for the best results.

Preserving Ripe Fruits for Future Use

Preserving ripe fruits allows you to enjoy their flavors long after their peak season has passed. Here are some effective methods for preserving and storing ripe fruits.

Canning

1. Jam and Jelly

- **Ingredients:** Ripe fruit, sugar, and pectin.
- **Instructions:** Cook ripe fruit with sugar and pectin to create a jam or jelly. Sterilize jars and process according to recommended canning procedures to ensure preservation.

2. Fruit Conserves

- **Ingredients:** Ripe fruit, sugar, nuts, and spices.
- **Instructions:** Combine fruit with sugar, nuts, and spices to create a fruit conserve. Cook until thickened, then can as you would with jam.

Freezing

1. Flash Freezing

- **Ingredients:** Ripe fruit, such as berries or sliced peaches.
- **Instructions:** Spread fruit in a single layer on a baking sheet and freeze until solid. Transfer to freezer bags or containers for long-term storage.

2. Frozen Fruit Cubes

- **Ingredients:** Ripe fruit and water or juice.
- **Instructions:** Puree ripe fruit and freeze in ice cube trays. Use fruit cubes in smoothies or as a refreshing addition to beverages.

Dehydrating

1. Dried Fruit Snacks

- **Ingredients:** Ripe fruit, such as apples, pears, or apricots.
- **Instructions:** Slice fruit thinly and dehydrate using a dehydrator or oven at a low temperature. Store in airtight containers for long-term use.

2. Fruit Leathers

- **Ingredients:** Pureed ripe fruit.
- **Instructions:** Spread fruit puree onto dehydrator trays or baking sheets and dehydrate until leathery. Roll up and store in airtight containers.

Tips for Preserving Ripe Fruits

- **Proper Storage:** Use airtight containers or vacuum-sealed bags for freezing and dehydrated fruits to prevent freezer burn or spoilage.
- **Labeling:** Clearly label preserved fruits with the date to keep track of freshness and use within recommended time frames.
- **Check for Ripeness:** Ensure fruits are perfectly ripe before preserving to achieve the best flavor and texture.

Creative Ideas for Serving and Presentation

The way you present fruit-based dishes can elevate their appeal and make them more enjoyable. Here are some creative ideas for serving and presenting ripe fruits and fruit-based dishes.

Fruit Platters

- **Seasonal Arrangements:** Create fruit platters with a variety of colors and textures. Arrange fruits in a visually pleasing manner, incorporating seasonal favorites.

- **Themed Platters:** Design platters around themes, such as tropical fruits for a summer party or a mix of autumn fruits for a harvest celebration.

Fruit Salads

- **Colorful Creations:** Mix different types of ripe fruit into a vibrant salad. Add a splash of citrus juice or a drizzle of honey for extra flavor.
- **Add-ins:** Enhance fruit salads with nuts, seeds, or fresh herbs like mint for added texture and flavor.

Elegant Desserts

- **Fruit Parfaits:** Layer ripe fruit with yogurt and granola in clear glasses for a visually appealing and tasty treat.
- **Fruit Tarts:** Garnish fruit tarts with a glossy fruit glaze or a sprinkle of powdered sugar for an elegant presentation.

Tips for Presentation

- **Use Fresh Herbs:** Garnish dishes with fresh herbs like mint or basil for added color and flavor.
- **Glassware and Plates:** Use clear glassware or elegant plates to highlight the vibrant colors and textures of your fruit-based dishes.
- **Creative Garnishes:** Incorporate edible flowers or zest for a sophisticated touch.

Conclusion

Harnessing the full potential of ripe fruits through creative recipes and preservation techniques allows you to enjoy their peak flavors all year round. Whether you're blending them into refreshing smoothies, baking them into delightful desserts, or preserving them for future use, ripe fruits offer a world of culinary possibilities. By employing these ideas and techniques, you can celebrate the natural sweetness and versatility of fruits, turning them into memorable dishes that delight the senses. Embrace the art of working with ripe fruits and let your culinary creativity shine.

10 Mastering the Art of Ripening: A Comprehensive Recap and Final Insights

As we reach the culmination of our exploration into the art of ripening fruits, it's essential to reflect on the journey we've undertaken. From understanding the science behind ripening to applying practical strategies for optimal fruit storage and use, this chapter aims to recap the key concepts, highlight the benefits of controlled ripening, and encourage further experimentation and personal discovery. Whether you're a dedicated home cook, a passionate gardener, or a curious food enthusiast, this final chapter will reinforce the principles we've discussed and inspire you to take your fruit ripening skills to new heights.

Recap of Key Concepts

Understanding Ripening Dynamics

Ripening is a complex process involving biochemical changes that transform fruits from hard and inedible to soft, sweet, and flavorful. The ripening process is driven by ethylene, a natural plant hormone, which accelerates the breakdown of starches into sugars and the softening of fruit tissues. Recognizing the two primary categories of fruits—climacteric and non-climacteric—has been fundamental. Climacteric fruits, such as apples and bananas, continue to ripen after harvest due to their production of ethylene. In contrast, non-climacteric fruits, such as strawberries and grapes, reach their peak ripeness at harvest and do not benefit from additional ethylene exposure.

Strategic Pairing for Optimal Ripening

Effective fruit ripening often involves strategic pairing. For instance, placing bananas with avocados can speed up the ripening of both fruits due to the ethylene emitted by bananas. Conversely, certain pairings, such as storing apples with leafy greens, can lead to accelerated spoilage due to the ethylene-induced aging effects. Understanding these interactions has been crucial for optimizing fruit ripeness and avoiding over-ripening.

Storage Techniques and Preservation

We've explored various methods for storing ripe fruits, including traditional techniques like using paper bags and modern tools such as controlled atmosphere storage. Paper bags can help concentrate ethylene around climacteric fruits, while controlled atmosphere storage adjusts oxygen and carbon dioxide levels to extend freshness. Additionally, freezing and canning offer methods for preserving ripe fruits, allowing you to enjoy seasonal flavors year-round.

Creative Uses for Ripe Fruits

Our journey also included creative applications for ripe fruits, from smoothies and natural juices to elegant desserts and preserved treats. Ripe fruits can be transformed into delightful smoothies that capture their peak sweetness, or used in desserts like fruit tarts and cobblers that celebrate their natural flavors. Preservation methods like freezing and canning ensure that you can savor the essence of ripe fruits long after their season has ended.

Benefits of Controlled Fruit Ripening

Enhanced Flavor and Quality

Controlled ripening allows for the optimal development of fruit flavors and textures. By managing the ripening environment, such as temperature and ethylene levels, you can ensure that fruits reach their peak sweetness and juiciness. This not only enhances the eating experience but also maximizes the nutritional value of the fruit.

Reduced Waste and Increased Efficiency

Understanding and controlling the ripening process helps reduce food waste. By timing the ripening of fruits to match consumption patterns, you can prevent spoilage and ensure that fruits are enjoyed at their best. Additionally, strategic ripening and storage can lead to more efficient use of resources, whether you're managing a garden or a household fruit supply.

Flexibility and Convenience

Controlled ripening methods provide flexibility and convenience, especially for those who wish to enjoy seasonal fruits out of their natural harvest time. Techniques like freezing and canning allow you to preserve fruits at their peak ripeness, making them available for use throughout the year. This versatility is invaluable for creating diverse dishes and managing your fruit inventory effectively.

Economic and Environmental Benefits

By reducing waste and extending the shelf life of fruits, controlled ripening can offer economic benefits. Fewer spoiled fruits mean cost savings and better utilization of purchased produce. Environmentally, reducing food waste contributes to a lower carbon footprint and a more sustainable approach to consumption.

Encouragement for Experimentation and Personal Discovery

Embrace the Art of Ripening

While the science of fruit ripening provides a solid foundation, the art of ripening is where personal creativity and experimentation come into play. Each fruit and ripening scenario is unique, and discovering what works best for you requires a willingness to experiment. Whether you're trying new pairings, testing different storage methods, or crafting your own fruit-based recipes, the process of exploration can lead to delightful surprises and improved results.

Keep a Ripening Journal

Consider keeping a ripening journal to track your observations and results. Documenting your experiments with different fruits, pairings, and storage techniques will help you refine your approach and build a personalized guide for optimal ripening. Include details such as ripening times, flavor notes, and any challenges you encounter.

Share and Learn from Others

Engage with fellow fruit enthusiasts, gardeners, and home cooks to share your experiences and learn from others. Participating in community forums, attending workshops, or joining local fruit preservation groups can provide valuable insights and inspire new ideas. Collaborative learning can enhance your ripening techniques and expand your culinary repertoire.

Adapt and Innovate

Feel free to adapt traditional methods to suit your preferences and lifestyle. Innovation is key to mastering the art of ripening, and experimenting with new techniques or combining different approaches can lead to unique and successful outcomes. Be open to adjusting your methods based on seasonal variations, fruit types, and personal preferences.

Conclusion

Mastering the art of ripening fruits is both a science and an art, combining knowledge with creativity to achieve the best flavors and textures. By understanding the principles of ripening, applying strategic pairing and storage techniques, and exploring creative uses for ripe fruits, you can elevate your culinary experiences and make the most of your fruit harvests. As you continue to experiment and discover what works best for you, remember that the journey of ripening fruits is an ongoing adventure. Embrace the process, enjoy the results, and let your love for perfectly ripe fruits inspire your culinary creations.

www.ingramcontent.com/pod-product-compliance
Lightning Source LLC
Chambersburg PA
CBHW070007060125
19960CB00014B/2186